Look at the tails!

Written by Susan Frame

a Capstone company — publishers for children

A cat has a tail. A dog has one, too. Cockatoos and bats have tails. And a pig has a tail with a curl in it.

Let's have a look at tails – the things they can do and the things they can tell us.

Cat tails

A cat can puff out the fur on her tail, so she looks bigger. This tells us she is going to fight!

A tail up in the air tells you that a cat feels secure.

If you are patting a cat, he might purr and wag his tail a bit. Yes, a cat will wag his tail to tell you he feels good.

But a cat might wag his tail to tell you he is upset, too. That's odd!

This is a bobtail cat. Can you see its tail? It has a short one.

And this cat has no tail at all.

Do you think a cat looks better with a tail or with no tail?

Dog tails

If a dog's tail is up in the air and wagging, the dog is feeling good.

If a dog's tail is down or is tucked in its back legs, the dog is telling you, "I do not feel good. Back off!"

If a dog has her tail down but she wags it a bit, she is telling you that a pat might be good for her right now.

Cockatoo tails

A cockatoo wags his tail to tell you he feels good as he sits in the sun.

But if he fans his tail out, he is telling you to back off.

His tail gets him high up, up, up into the air. His tail lets him turn in the air, too.

Bat tails

Look at the tail on a short-tailed bat. The bat wags its short tail to get up into the air.

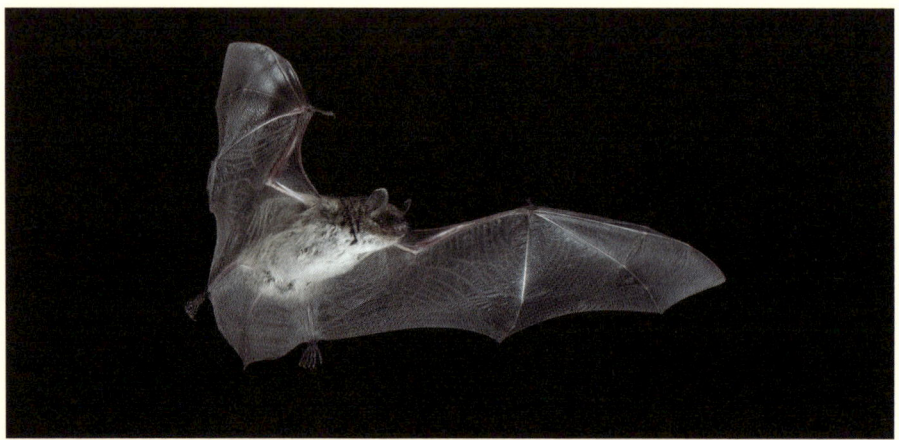

This is a long-tailed bat. This bat can feel things to the rear of it with its tail.

This bat has a short tail, but **long** ears!

Pig tails

A pig's tail is short. It has a curl and a bit of hair at the tip of it.
If a pig's tail is not in a curl, it tells us that she might be unwell.
The farmer will need to get a vet to see her so she can get better.

Shoo! If things are on its back, this pig can shoo them off with its tail.

Tails, tails, tails. A shark has a tail. A lizard has one. Arctic foxes and rats have thick tails.

Shark tails

A shark's tail is a fin. This fin has a long bit and a short bit.

This sort of shark has a long, long tail fin. If the shark sees a shoal of fish, it hits them with its tail fin. Now it can feed on fish for its dinner.

Lizard tails

A lizard's tail keeps the lizard level as it zooms along the soil.

This sort of lizard has a big curl in its tail. It looks cool.

A lizard's tail has 'pillars' in it. The pillars fit into sockets. If a lizard is in a fight, the pillars can pop out of the sockets. Then, the lizard sheds its tail and runs off. It will not be dinner for now.

This lizard had to shed its tail. Its tail is back now, but much shorter than it was.

Arctic fox tail

This Arctic fox has thick fur on its tail. This is good for the fox. You can see how its tail curls up to its chin and keeps out the chill.

If the fox sees a lemming, it might think, "Food!"
With its tail out at the rear, it runs.
Look out, lemming. This fox is quick.

This is a lemming.

Rat tails

This rat's tail is thick. A rat's tail might look hairless, but it has lots of short hairs on it. The hairs are so thin that they are hard for us to see.

A rat needs a tail. Its long tail cools the rat down if it gets too hot. So, if a cat gets a rat's tail, it is not good for the rat at all. It can get sick if it has no tail.

Ow! It hurts a lot to be picked up by the tail. So do not do that to a rat, thank you! This is much better.

There are all sorts of tails. Pick one that you think looks good.

Look at the tails! They tell us all sorts of things.

How do I feel?

24